NEW ENGLAND VILLAGE

NEW ENGLAND VILLAGE

Everyday Life in 1810

BY ROBERT H. LOEB, JR.

Doubleday & Company, Inc., Garden City, New York

DESIGNED BY LAURENCE ALEXANDER

ISBN: 0-385-11488-5 Trade
       0-385-11489-3 Prebound
Library of Congress Catalog Card Number 76–2791

ACKNOWLEDGMENTS

I wish to thank the staff of Old Sturbridge Village, Massachusetts, for the use of their excellent research library, and for their co-operation in checking the text for historical accuracy.

My thanks are also extended to The Old Slater Mill Museum, Pawtucket, Rhode Island, and to its curator, Gary Kulik. He provided me with most of the data pertaining to the operational and social conditions involved in mill work.

PHOTO CREDITS:
OLD STURBRIDGE VILLAGE: pages xii, 3, 5, 8, 15, 17, 23, 26, 27, 28, 29, 31, 32, 33, 36, 39, 49, 51, 53, 55.
JAY CANTOR: pages 6, 7, 13, 20, 37, 59.
OLD SLATER MILL MUSEUM: pages 71, 75, 76.

CONTENTS

INTRODUCTION

The village we are about to visit in New England, to see what life was like in 1810, does not actually exist. It's what a typical village might have been like in those days. However, the descriptions and pictures of how such a village looked are, in good part, based upon one which does exist today: Old Sturbridge Village. It is located in Sturbridge, Massachusetts, and all the homes, farmhouses, and other buildings in that village date back to early days. They were moved there from various parts of New England. People come from all over the country to visit this large outdoor museum.

The Old Slater Mill, which we are also going to visit, actually exists where it was located back in 1810. Today, it too is a museum, located in Pawtucket, Rhode Island, and can be visited.

NEW ENGLAND VILLAGE

Bird's-eye view of village

CHAPTER 1

Welcome to the Village

Can you imagine what life was like in a New England village almost one hundred and seventy years ago? You don't have to guess, because I'm going to take you there: on a journey back in time to a New England village in 1810. That's when the United States was far smaller than it is today. There were only nineteen states and five territories. James Madison, who had succeeded Thomas Jefferson only one year earlier, was the country's fourth President. Fulton's steamboat had recently made its first successful voyage.

This is what the village looks like from a bird's-eye view. The large patch of lawn, which is called the village green, is surrounded by different kinds of buildings: homes, the church, the village store, and various craftsmen's shops. In the distance are the farmhouses and barns. Almost all of the villagers depend upon farming for their living. Even the minister, the tinsmith, the blacksmith, the potter, and the village lawyer are also farmers.

The village probably looks quite small to you. And it is, compared to what you and I are used to. There are only a little more than two hundred families living here, but it's an average-size village for the times. There are very few cities throughout the country, and Boston, the largest city in Massachusetts, has only 33,250 inhabitants. Compare this to the metropolitan Boston of our time, which has almost three million people. That figure would be almost impossible for the villagers to grasp, as there were only six million inhabitants in the entire country in 1810.

Here is what the village looks like as we approach the green. Yes, it's quiet and peaceful, or so it must seem to you. There are no cars, trucks, or motorcycles whizzing and screeching about. During our entire stay we won't even see a bicycle. When people want to go from here to there, they either walk or go by oxcart. Very few even have horses. And there's nothing flying about in the sky except birds—no jets or other airplanes. This limits the scope of travel a good deal. But notice how clean and fresh the air is. There are no exhaust fumes to pollute it.

On another day we'll explore the craftsmen's shops and the village store. But now let's be on our way to

The village green

the farmhouse, just outside the village proper, where you'll stay and share village life. I must caution you, however, that it won't be all fun. And certainly not make-believe. Some of the things you may experience in the village may strike you as disappointing and sometimes even uncomfortable. But when you're all through with your visit and return to our modern world, you'll see that, though there are many disadvantages to this way of life, there are also advantages which you and I might envy.

CHAPTER 2

Make Yourself at Home

There's the farmhouse up ahead. The villagers have just had their first winter snowfall and the first real spell of cold weather. When you enter the farmhouse, you won't find it as warm as you might hope. The fireplace is the only source of heat, and you'll have to get up close to it to get warm. Sad to say, most of the heat from the fire goes up the chimney, so that the rest of the room is as cold and drafty as a cave. On a very cold day it's not uncommon for a pan of water, just a few feet away from the fireplace, to be coated with ice. This house, one of the newer ones built in 1801, does have four fireplaces. But it has six rooms, which means that two of them are unheated.

The kitchen is an all-purpose room, where the family does their cooking, eating, and much of their

Farmhouse

living. Some members of the family sleep here as well, because it's the warmest room in the house. All the cooking is done in the fireplace, including pies and bread. They're baked in the brick oven, the deep cubbyhole at the side of the fireplace. Hot coals are placed in the oven to bring it to the right baking temperature.

Right off the kitchen is the buttery. As you've guessed, it's where butter is made, as well as cheese. The other end of the kitchen opens onto two other rooms. One is used as a dining room on special

Brick oven

occasions, on holidays and for entertaining important people, such as the minister or village lawyer. The other room is used for everyday living. It's the family's room and gives them a place, other than the kitchen, in which to sit and sleep. A steep, narrow stairway leads to two small bedrooms upstairs, only one of which has a fireplace. Perhaps you'll be lucky enough to sleep in that one tonight.

"But," you're possibly wondering, yet embarrassed to ask, "where are the bathrooms?"

Fireplace

To answer that, you'll have to come outside the house and see where the *privy* is. It's a little wooden shed, which serves as a toilet facility. No, it's not exactly comfortable to get to, especially on a cold winter night, or when it's snowing or raining. Even though the homes of some wealthy families have many more rooms and much fancier furniture, not one of them has such a thing as a bath or indoor toilet. There's simply no plumbing in any of the homes. This house is quite exceptional, as it has a spring in the buttery, which means there is water constantly flowing into the sink. But the other villagers depend upon wells, outside the house, for their water supply. This means that the water has to be carted in by the bucketful, not exactly a delightful chore. In the winter the top of the well sometimes freezes over. Then the oxen have to be hitched up to the sled and water fetched from the stream down the road.

As for hot water, it's such a luxury, since it has to be heated over the fire, that the villagers do their laundry only once or twice a month and, compared to our standards, bathe infrequently. As a result, they may smell a bit at times, and fleas are not uncommon. But since they are all in the same condition, they don't really notice it, and they do try to keep as clean as possible. And consider this: our craze for washing machines, dishwashers, and two baths in every home is one reason for our problem of water pollution. Perhaps this is a high price to pay for such comforts.

The buttery

Now that you've seen *where* the family lives, it's time to acquaint you with *how* they live—what family life is like. The house is small, considering how many are living in it: the parents, four children, the father's parents, and the mother's sister. You can readily see that there's not much individual privacy, but they manage to get along. Everyone, regardless of age, shares in the work that has to be done.

Parents raise large families and like to have many more children than most people have in our time. This is not only because they love children, but for some practical reasons as well. The more children they have, the more helping hands there are to share the work. Even the tiniest hands can do useful things.

The other reason for having large families may be upsetting, but I insist on being truthful. The unpleasant fact is that, because medical knowledge is so limited, many infants die in childbirth. Furthermore, young children, along with adults, often die of sicknesses for which there are no cures. People need to have large families to make up for those who die of illness.

I should also prepare you for what the villagers expect of children and how they're to behave. A parent's word is law, especially the father's. He expects complete obedience and brooks no arguments or backtalk. In other words, parents in 1810 are very strict compared to our standards. Children must learn the difference between right and wrong from their elders and, of course, from the teachings of the Bible, which they read when very young.

People don't pamper or spoil their children. They teach them to look upon idleness as sin and work as blessed. They believe that a child who's lazy or disobedient, and who disregards the teachings of the Scripture, will more than likely become a criminal.

This may surprise you, too: they believe that women are not as capable of thinking things through and of making correct decisions as men. This is why they do not allow them to vote, or even to talk at town or church meetings, although I believe exceptions are sometimes made.

Life for most of them is a hard struggle. They have to face droughts, floods, and other disasters which threaten their crops and livestock. Sickness, serious accidents (which are quite common), and frequent deaths are very much a part of their daily lives. Consequently, they depend upon a strong religious faith to face such unpleasant things. Unfortunately, many are intolerant of those outside their faith and of people with differently colored skin. Far more so than most of us are today.

However, despite the hardships they have to face, they also have some advantages which we do not have. Their countryside is still unspoiled, the air fresh, and the streams and ponds and lakes are untouched by pollution. So, despite all the work they have to do, these are pleasures their children can enjoy.

I hope, therefore, that you'll look forward to tomorrow and enjoy sharing their way of life.

CHAPTER 3

A Day of Work at Home

The fire's burning in the kitchen and the family is about to have breakfast. So slip on your clothes and join them. There's a kettle filled with water near the fire, so you can wash your hands and face.

The family always starts off the day with a hearty breakfast to fuel up for the long day's work ahead. However, don't expect the kind of breakfast you're accustomed to. You'll find much of the food they eat quite different from ours. Recently, a foreigner from a large European city visited New England and described a farm breakfast in his diary like this:

> "The morning at breakfast they deluge their stomachs with a quart of hot water, impregnated with tea, or so slightly with coffee that it is mere colored water, and they swallow, almost without chewing, hot bread, half baked, toast soaked in butter, cheese of the fattest kind, slices of salt or hung beef, ham, etc., all of which is nearly insoluble."

Kettle

That doesn't sound very appetizing. And perhaps it's an unfair description. The villagers do brew weak coffee and tea. But coffee beans and tea leaves have to be purchased at the village store and are expensive. And since wheat doesn't grow well in their kind of soil and climate, they make bread from their own crops of rye and Indian corn. Undoubtedly, it tastes different from bread made of wheat flour, but the farmers make do with what they raise. They make no apology for serving lots of meat, butter and homemade cheeses at breakfast. As far as they're concerned, meat is man's most important food. They even feed it to babies who haven't even their first teeth.

When breakfast is over, the menfolk go out to tend to their farm chores. The tiny children, women and girls stay indoors to start their work. And what a variety of things they have to do to keep the family fed, clothed, and comfortable.

MAKING BUTTER AND CHEESE

One of the older girls is about to make butter. Butter, as you know, is made from cream, which, in turn, comes from milk. First the milk is strained through a cloth to remove impurities. Then, in order to separate the cream from the milk, it's poured into large tin or pottery pans. In the wintertime these containers are placed near the fireplace for a day or a day and a half. In the summer it takes only about eight hours for the cream to rise to the top. Then it's scooped out

Churning butter

with a skimmer and put into the churn. The plunger has to be pushed up and down, without stopping, for at least half an hour before the lump of butter forms. The liquid that is left, called buttermilk, is poured off. The butter is then washed and squeezed under cold water to rid it of any remaining liquid. At the same time, salt is worked into the butter to keep it from turning rancid—always a problem in warm weather, since there is no refrigeration.

Now let's see how cheese is made. When you were a little child you undoubtedly heard this nursery rhyme: "Little Miss Muffet sat on a tuffet eating her curds and whey, when along came a spider . . ." and so on. A tuffet is a low stool and has nothing to do with cheese making. But curds and whey, which come from milk, do. Changing milk into curds and whey is the first step in making cheese, and it is not nearly as simple as separating the cream.

The fresh milk is poured into large crocks and set in front of the fire for about an hour—or as long as it takes for it to reach the correct temperature, 96° F. The woman can test the temperature without using a thermometer. Through years of experience she's learned to feel when the milk is warm enough.

At this point *rennet* is added. Rennet, which looks like fine strips of leather, comes from the lining of an unweaned calf's stomach. Almost from the moment the rennet is added, a great change takes place in the milk. And at the end of about forty-five minutes, there's no milk at all: just curds and whey. The lumpy parts are

Pouring off buttermilk

the curds, and the watery part is the whey. The curds are separated out by straining the mixture through a cloth. Then the woman works the curds with her hands to squeeze out more whey. At the same time she adds salt. The final step is to place the salted curds in a shallow wooden pan, which is then put under the cheese press. The press squeezes out all the remaining liquid. After the cheese is taken out of the wooden pan it resembles a small wheel, and it's stored in a cool place so that it ages. The longer the cheese is allowed to sit, the sharper tasting it becomes.

Cheese keeps far longer and better than butter, which is why the family makes so much of it. But it takes a great quantity of milk to make a comparatively small amount of cheese. You may have noticed that there was no milk at breakfast. Very little milk is ever served, even to children. There are good reasons for this. In the spring and summer, when the cows are yielding a good supply, there is no way of keeping the milk cool so that it won't sour. The most sensible thing is to make it into butter and cheese, which keep better. Furthermore, when cold weather sets in and the grass in the pastures yellows and dies out, the dairy cattle give very little milk because there's so little for them to eat.

You can now understand why milk is rarely served at mealtime and why families rely on beverages such as cider, coffee and tea. And, as far as they're concerned, children get along without it. Some of our food scientists, or nutritionists, claim that the lack of milk, leafy vegetables and fresh fruits in their diet had some bad effects. They say it explains why so many of them had poor teeth at an early age and why their average height is far less than ours. This is probably so. But let's not forget that, with all our scientific knowledge, we have nutritional problems of our own making. We consume far more sugar than is good for us. Worse yet, many of our foods are preserved with harmful chemicals and often colored with dyes which can cause serious problems. And saddest of all, despite all the foods we're able to grow, store, freeze and preserve, there are millions who still aren't getting enough to eat.

PREPARING THE MEALS

Now let's go into the kitchen. Just cooking three meals a day for so large a family is no small task. When the men and boys return from the fields at noontime, their appetites will be enormous after all their outdoor work. That's why the midday meal, which is the family's dinner, is already being cooked.

Fireplace cookery is quite an undertaking from beginning to end. Just tending the fire and keeping it stoked with wood requires a lot of effort. Starting the fire, should it go out during the night, is no simple feat. Striking a flame with a tinderbox, which consists of flint, steel and an oil-soaked rag, can take hundreds of tries. In fact, it's often simpler to send one of the boys to a neighbor's house to bring back some hot coals.

Tinderbox

Heavy iron kettle

The cooking itself is strictly the girls' and women's task, and it requires considerable strength. As a rule, they cook all the vegetables together in a heavy iron kettle. Even when empty it weighs almost forty pounds. You can imagine how heavy it is when filled and how much strength it takes to put it on and take it off the fire.

The main vegetables which are cooked together are turnips, pumpkins, beans, and dried peas. Potatoes are cooked separately in a wrought-iron potato boiler. The choice of vegetables is limited chiefly to those because they can be dried or stored in a cool place and kept throughout the winter and early spring.

By late spring and summer the family can hope to enjoy fresh green vegetables from the kitchen garden. But this is sometimes more of a hope than a reality. The women have so much other work to do that tending the kitchen garden, which is their job, is often neglected.

On the other hand, strawberries and raspberries grow wild all over the countryside, and apple and peach trees are quite common. Unfortunately, however, people can enjoy the fresh-picked berries and peaches only while they're in season. To be sure, they know how to preserve them, but that requires lots of sugar, and sugar is too costly for them to use in such a manner. Instead they use molasses, which is far cheaper, or maple sugar which they make themselves, for most of their sweetening.

One of the girls has gone out to the barnyard to

gather eggs. Finding the eggs is much like an Easter egg hunt, because the hens are allowed to roam all over and there's no telling where the eggs will be laid. Also, the hens don't lay nearly as many eggs as the family might like. As a result, the family can't afford to serve eggs at breakfast, or as a separate food at any meal, but uses them only in baking.

You are probably curious to know what foods you will be served at mealtime. Among the most common dishes are broth, and pork mixed with cornmeal. Dessert often consists of hasty pudding, which is made from cornmeal mush, sweetened with maple sugar or molasses, and served with milk.

To be truthful, everyday meals are quite limited in variety and perhaps even monotonous. But on feast days, especially Thanksgiving, families go all out.

We've spent so much time on food preparation, you'd think that's all that went on in the household, which is far from the case.

MAKING CANDLES AND SOAP

Although some homes are beginning to use oil lamps for lighting, this family and many others depend upon candles. But the candles weren't bought at the store. Instead, they're made right here at home. For daily use the candles are made from tallow and, when lit, smell a bit like frying grease. That's because tallow is made from rendered animal fat. In order to make

Dipping candles

these candles, the wicks are dipped into hot, melted tallow time after time. In between each dipping they are hung up to cool so that the tallow coating hardens. When there's time, candles are made out of the wax from bayberries. These candles give off a most pleasing scent and are only used on special occasions.

Soap is also homemade. Soapmaking is a rather time-consuming process, which requires boiling tallow and wood ash in a huge iron pot. However, even this is a minor undertaking compared to the making of cloth, which the family needs for clothing, blankets, sheets, towels, curtains and many other items.

MAKING CLOTH

I want to describe clothmaking to you in some detail. It will show not only how self-reliant most of the villagers are, but the tremendous amount of time and work that's required for a family like this one to live in even modest comfort.

Over the past ten years, factories have started up in New England towns which can actually spin cotton thread by machines. In fact, some of this thread is for sale in the village store. But few can afford to buy it. And, although cotton is coming into use more and more, most of the villagers choose to stick to what they have at hand: wool and flax. To be sure, wealthy families, especially those living in the large towns and cities, buy silk, satin, velvet and cotton fabrics, and even pay dressmakers and tailors to make their fancy clothing.

But for most of these villagers such luxuries are out of the question.

The average family makes about a hundred yards of cloth per year. Spinning thread and weaving it into cloth on handlooms involves a tremendous amount of time and labor. But almost as much work is required just to get the wool and flax ready for spinning.

Preparing Flax and Wool

The flax plants, from which linen is made, are planted in the spring. Before they fully ripen, usually in July, the farmer has to pull up each stalk by the roots. The stalks are carefully tied into small bundles and allowed to lie on the ground for a few days until the seeds ripen. Then the seeds are removed by drawing the stalks through a *ripple,* which resembles an iron comb. The seeds are kept for the next year's planting. The seedless stalks are first soaked in water and then allowed to dry. Once again they have to be gathered and tied into small bundles. In order to separate the fiber from the rough outside covering, each bundle is placed under a *brake,* which resembles a long wooden knife. The brake strips off the bark from the fiber.

By now you're probably muttering, "Enough. Let's get to spinning and weaving."

But we're not ready yet. Next the fibers have to be straightened out, and the coarse ones separated from the fine ones. This is accomplished by drawing them through a *hackle* (sometimes called a *heckle*). This is

Brake for flax

a wooden board studded with fine iron teeth. The coarse fibers, which are caught in the hackle, are often used for making rope. The fine ones are finally ready to be spun into linen threads.

Preparing wool for spinning is every bit as complicated as flax. First the farmer has to shear the sheep. This is done in the springtime when the animals no longer need their thick, heavy coats of wool to keep them warm.

Ripple for flax

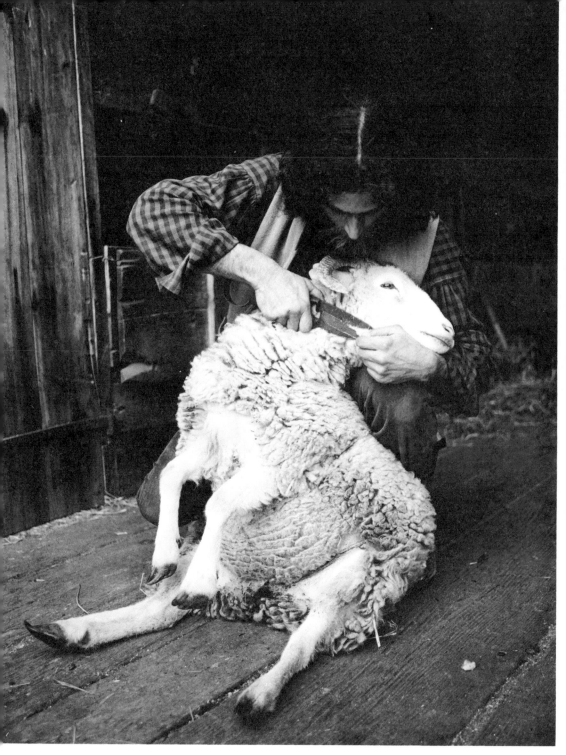

Shearing a sheep

Hand carding wool

Shearing sheep requires skill and practice. No one's ever come across a lamb who'd stay still like someone in a barber's chair. Unfortunately, too, sheep neither wash nor bathe, so that their wool is full of twigs, burrs, dirt and oil. The shorn wool has to be cleaned, which the family does by washing it in warm water and soap. Then it's spread in the grass in a shady place to dry. After that, the entire family works over the wool to pull out the burrs and twigs.

At this point the cleaned wool is in a rather tangled mess and needs straightening out and fluffing up before it can be spun. This is done by *carding* it. Not too long ago, carding was done at home by hand. But now there is a carding mill in the village.

Let's go along with the girls who are about to take a basketful of wool into the village to be carded. The mill is located beside a stream and is run by waterpower.

The machine-operated carder draws the tangled wool, by means of a series of rollers, through fine iron bristles. The wool comes out all soft and fluffy.

The mill owner doesn't card the wool for fun. He expects to be paid, but not necessarily with money. In this instance the farmer arranged to deliver some bushels of rye, when they're harvested, in exchange for his services.

Spinning Thread

Now it's time to hurry back, as the grandmother is impatient to start her spinning. The spinning wheel she is using is turned by working the foot treadle, which is linked by a pulley to the spindles. They twist the fluffy wool into thread. Watching a practiced spinner may make the process look quite easy. However, it takes skill, concentration and, above all, patience and endurance.

This treadle spinning wheel is a great improvement over the one she used to use. The old-time spinning wheel, which she still uses occasionally, is called the *high wheel* (or wool wheel). It has no foot treadle. Consequently, the wheel has to be turned by hand, first forward, then backward. The operator has to step back and forth to alternate the turns and guide the

Spinning wool with treadle spinning wheel

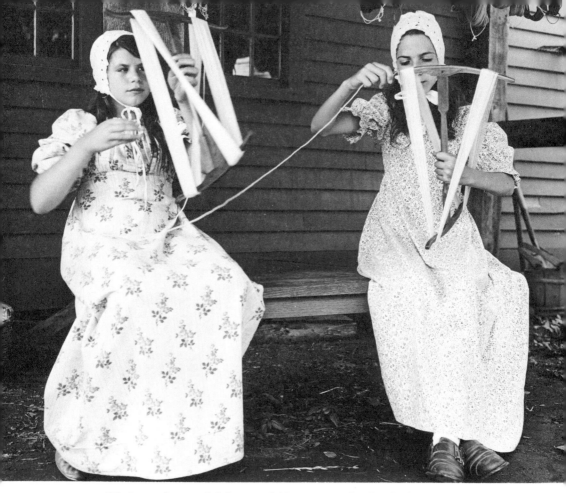

Girls using niddy-noddies to wind skeins

wool onto the spindles. Grandmother has said that there were days when she may have walked almost twenty miles working the high wheel!

Winding Skeins

Later this afternoon, and certainly by early evening, there will be enough spun thread so that the children can take turns winding it into skeins. This is done by winding it on a *reel*. Forty turns of the reel must be

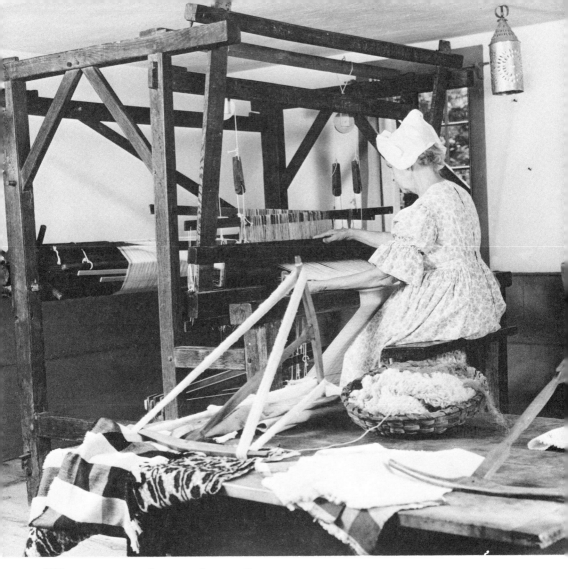

Woman weaving on home loom

carefully counted off so that each skein is the same length.

Sometimes, when more thread has been spun than can be handled on the reel, a hand reel is also used. It's called a *niddy-noddy,* and it's swung around until forty turns are made. I can promise you that if you try using the niddy-noddy after supper for an hour or two, you'll be glad to go to bed.

Once the thread is wound into skeins, it is dyed and sometimes bleached. Indigo is used for a blue color, but it has to be bought at the store. It comes from the indigo plant, which grows only in warm climates and comes from the South. Native plants, such as pokeberries, madder, goldenrod, hickory, butternut, and sassafras bark are used for other colors.

After all the time and effort that has gone into preparing the thread, one might hope that at least the weaving process would be fast and easy. But, if anything, operating the family loom requires even more skill. You can imagine how much cloth is needed to keep a whole family clothed and warm.

As you've now seen, this home is not just a place to live. It is a kind of miniature factory which turns out almost all the family's necessities.

CHAPTER 4

Working the Farm

The sky is pink with the promise of a beautiful spring day, and the menfolk are going out to prepare the fields for planting. Let's join them at the barn. As you can see, it's a solidly built structure. It's as important to the farmer as his house. It serves as shelter for livestock, and as storage space for farm tools and hay. In the center is the threshing floor. In the fall, after the grain crops have been harvested, they're brought here and the grain is separated from the stalks by beating them with a flail.

The stalls for the cows and oxen line both sides of the threshing floor. However, the animals are kept inside only from late fall to early summer. The remainder of the time they are turned out to pasture. The corn is stored in the corn crib nearby.

The barn

Empty corn crib, raised on stilts to keep out animals

Each of the farmers in the village owns between one hundred and two hundred acres of land. This farm is among the larger ones. About one third of it is woodland, another third is pasture for the cattle, and most of the rest is mowing fields for hay. Only a very small part of it is used for planting crops—about ten acres. Because there is no place where a farmer can sell extra crops, he plants just enough for his own family to use.

Our farmer has ten cows, one yoke of oxen, fifteen sheep, and a dozen pigs. Few of the farmers own horses, which are far more expensive to buy than oxen, and also more expensive to feed. I don't doubt that some must envy those few farmers who keep horses and drive about so fast in their fancy buggies. But oxen, though they move slowly, can pull a good deal more and are more sure-footed on the rocky, hilly land of New England. Oxcarts are crude and cumbersome, but they serve quite well for transporting crops, timber, stone and hay. To cart very heavy loads for long distances, the farmers usually wait until winter, when there's snow on the ground, so they can use a sledge, or sleigh.

They're hitching the oxen to the plow, and while you and I walk along I'll have time to tell you more, since the field is a good distance away and the oxen move as slowly as snails.

Some English visitors, and even a few American statesmen, have said that the villagers' farming methods are not much more advanced than those

Plowing field with oxen

practiced two hundred years ago. They claim that most farmers in New England are either ignorant or simply refuse to use improved farming implements and the more advanced methods which have been practiced in England and in other parts of this country. In fact, the late President, George Washington, was among these critics. Though what he stated was unfortunately true, it's only fair to point out that he had the shameful advantage of using slaves to do his farm work. Furthermore, he was the wealthiest man in the entire land, so he could easily afford to experiment with improved farm implements and methods. As a matter of fact, there are some gentlemen farmers in New England who can afford to invest in newfangled farming. And those farmers who live near large towns and cities, and sell their surplus crops, can afford to do so. But since these villagers raise crops only for their own use, they make do with what equipment they have, although it does take a lot of doing.

For example, the Carey plow, which most of them use, is crude compared to the one-piece, cast-iron plow that was invented twenty years ago. The Carey plow, which is made mostly of wooden pieces, takes a great deal of strength to handle and is far more difficult for oxen to pull. That's why it takes two men and a yoke of oxen an entire day to plow one or two acres.

One critical gentleman has gone so far as to say that the average New England farmer, because his tools are so poor, could carry almost all his farm equipment on his back!

Once the men have finished plowing the field, the next step is to sow the seeds. Each seed has to be dropped into the furrow by hand, and you can well imagine all the walking back and forth it takes to plant just one acre. Then, once this is completed, the oxen pull the harrow across the field to further loosen the soil and, at the same time, cover the seeds. It's said that even the harrows are way behind the times, as they have wooden, rather than iron, teeth.

New England farmers are also criticized for not doing much in the way of fertilizing their fields. They know that when manure is spread on a patch of ground, the harvest is greater. But they have a limited amount of manure, since their cattle are stabled only a few months out of the year. And what little manure is collected then is not carefully protected from rain or snow. Furthermore, spreading manure takes a lot of time and work. Consequently, they confine fertilizing to cornfields, since Indian corn is their most important crop.

It's thanks to the Indians that they have this food on which they are so dependent. "When the oakleaf was as big as a mouse's ear" (meaning in the spring, when the new leaves are still tiny), the Indian women would plant corn by making a hole in the ground with a sharp stick. Then they dropped in four or five kernels of corn and sometimes a dead fish, or some other fertilizer. Although the villagers' way of planting is an improvement over the Indians', they are indebted to the Indians for their most important grain food.

Besides, they get double use from the cornfields, as pumpkin seeds are planted around the hills of corn. After the corn has been harvested and the stalks cut down, the pumpkins are easily gathered.

It's going to take an entire week to plow three acres and plant corn. In another few weeks our farmer will plant some fields of rye, barley and buckwheat in small amounts, and a small field of flax. Last year he grew a little tobacco, which, unfortunately, the men and older boys enjoy smoking, and he'll plant even more this spring. Though it's none of my business, I cannot help thinking that it would be far better if he grew peas, beans and turnips instead.

It would be pleasant indeed if, after the spring planting were done, they could spend the summer relaxing, hunting and fishing. Instead, the mowing fields have to be cut for hay, and it takes an entire day to cut one acre with a scythe. Then the hay has to be gathered and stored for what little fodder they give the livestock during the winter. Flax is harvested and processed in July, and trees have to be cut down so that there will be a supply of firewood to last the family through the long, cold winter. There's been some talk that, at the rate they've been cutting down their woodlands, there'll come a day when wood will be in short supply. In fact, some farmers in northern New England already have to import their firewood. However, most of the farmers feel that they'll never face such a problem.

What with all the work that has to be done during the summer, fall is upon them before they're ready. Then it's time to start harvesting. The grain crops, such as rye, have to be cut down with a *cradle,* which is no light task to swing back and forth, hour after hour.

Compared to the way our modern farms are operated with machines and chemical fertilizers, their methods seem inefficient. But our scientific farming has serious disadvantages, too. The overuse of chemicals to fertilize the soil and destroy insects is bad for the environment. Much of our beef cattle and poultry are fed chemicals to make them grow faster and fatter, and these chemicals can taint the meat.

Although these New England farmers have to keep busy from dawn to dusk to work their farms, there's a sense of satisfaction in being self-sufficient and independent. Their great worry is that, although every member of the family shares in the work, they're always badly in need of more hands. To show you how desperate they sometimes are, our farmer and another villager, who has a horse and buggy, are going to a neighboring town to attend a pauper auction. We'll go along, and on the way back we can visit the village craftsmen's shops and the village store.

CHAPTER 5

Visiting a Pauper Auction and the Village Shops

Most New Englanders call a pauper auction a *vendu*. It's the most common way they have of taking care of the poor and needy—homeless widows and children, people who are crippled, and old people who are handicapped by rheumatism or some other infirmity. Almost everyone feels that these unfortunate people, the paupers, must be taken care of in some way.

Some years ago it was found that a cheap way to provide for the needy was to pay villagers to take them into their homes. Usually after a town meeting, at which funds are raised for taking care of the poor, a pauper auction is held. Paupers are put on the auction block. However, unlike a regular auction where merchandise goes to the highest bidder, a pauper goes to the lowest bidder. In other words, to the bidder who offers to accept the least amount of money from the town to keep the pauper.

A villager who underbids the others does not do so, I'm sorry to admit, because he wishes to save the town money and at the same time help an unfortunate person. He does it because taking in a pauper is a way of getting cheap labor. Whether the auctioned pauper be a child, the village drunk, or an old person whose joints are stiffened with rheumatism, he or she can perform some kind of work.

The farmer and his neighbor are going to the *vendu* because they found out that, among the paupers to be auctioned, are a widow and her three children. Her husband died a while back. He had lots of debts, and she was left with no place to live and no way to support her family. If the farmers are successful in making the lowest bid, they've agreed to divide the family between them. One will take the mother and one son; the other, the daughter and the youngest boy. The females will work in the house, and the males will work on the farm.

The *vendu* is being held at the inn, and the town is providing free drinks to all the people who attend. This lends a happy mood to a rather sorry occasion and sometimes helps liven up the bidding. You'll find the way the auctioneer describes the paupers quite shocking—very much like the inhuman slave auctions held in the South. Families are sometimes broken up and, worse yet, there's no telling how the paupers will be treated. You can see that the prospect is usually tragic for anyone who must depend on this form of charity.

To give you a feel of what a pauper auction is like, here is how someone described his experience.

He was riding through town when he saw sixty or seventy townsfolk gathered about the auctioneer. There were some pitiful-looking people huddled on the poorbench. Out of curiosity he dismounted and took in the sight.

The auctioneer called upon one of the paupers to get off the bench. She was a poor old woman who could barely stand up, she was so weak from hunger. The auctioneer, a cruel and heartless man, immediately started making fun of her. "Exhibit B for beauty," he said laughingly to the onlookers. Then he took her chin between thumb and forefinger and pulled down her jaw.

"Look, no teeth. Can't eat. She's cheap to feed. What's the offer?"

There were few bids but she was finally auctioned off. Several others were then auctioned off. Our observer was so depressed by the scene that he was about to leave. But the appearance of the next victim caught his attention. It was a little boy of eight or nine, as thin as a skeleton and dressed in rags. But he walked straight to the block with a look of defiance.

"How old are you, brat?" the auctioneer asked.

"Dunno."

"Come on, make a guess, young Web. That's your name, ain't it?" he added, consulting his auction list.

Then the auctioneer asked if he had any parents, and the boy replied no.

"Well, well, a foundling, huh? Nobody around to stir up trouble about you. That's good. And you don't know how old you are. Call it ten. How've you been living?"

The boy explained that he'd been working for a traveling circus but that it had gone out of business.

"So you get yourself on the poor list. Can you read?"

"No," the boy finally grunted.

"Well, I wouldn't expect it of you. Write nor figger, neither, I reckon."

The boy shook his head.

"See," the auctioneer announced gleefully. "No book learning to give him any fancy notions. A strong fellow, too. Strong and willing, ain't you boy?"

"Nope."

"Yes, you are," the auctioneer corrected as he cuffed him on the head. "Now, what's the bid on this one?"

The bidding became lively. The offers went lower and lower. One bidder, a large, ugly, cruel-looking man in a sailor's outfit, kept underbidding everyone. Our observer recognized him as a boat captain who had the reputation of being mean and brutish. He suddenly felt alarmed about the poor boy falling into his hands. The captain made his final bid saying, "Any man unders that, he'll have me to deal with."

There was a long silence. No one seemed to want to defy the captain. Suddenly the boy jumped from the platform and scrambled through the crowd. But he was caught and dragged back. There was such a look of fear and despair on his face that our observer called out, "I'll bid one dollar," much to his own amazement.

"One?" the auctioneer asked disbelievingly.

"One."

"Done," the auctioneer said. "Get down, boy. The next article is . . ."

Our observer made a beeline for his horse, with one eye out for the captain and one hand on the boy's collar. He swung into the saddle, and the boy jumped up behind him. The furious captain was pushing through the crowd toward them. There was no way of avoiding him, so the rider swung his horse around, set her straight at the captain, and bowled him over like a ninepin.

Our farmer is not attending this pauper's auction to rescue the widow and her children, but because he hopes to obtain additional help. However, I see that he and his friend have been underbid, so we'll head back to the village and I'll take you through some of the craftsmen's shops.

THE VILLAGE CRAFTSMEN

The Blacksmith

The blacksmith is probably the villagers' most important specialist. They depend on him for most of the tools they work with, iron rims for the wheels of carts

At the blacksmith's

and wagons, andirons and many of the utensils they use for cooking.

We need to be careful not to interrupt him or his helper, because as the saying goes, he must strike while the iron is hot. And look, that's exactly what he's doing. The sparks are flying about madly as he hammers away at the large piece of red-hot iron which he is shaping into the head of an axe. In contrast, you'll never guess what very tiny, but important, items he also makes: nails. Although machine-made nails can be bought at the village store, many people still prefer the blacksmith's handmade ones. He can bang out a solid, square-headed nail in less than a minute. In fact he's been known to turn one out in thirty-seven seconds.

By the way, he's called a blacksmith not because he's usually blackened with soot from his forge, which he is. It's because he works with iron, which is a black metal. Just as a tinsmith is often called a whitesmith because he works with a whitish metal.

The Tinsmith

This is the tinsmith's shop. Now that the tinsmith has a new machine, which saves him a good deal of hand hammering and time, he is manufacturing many more useful utensils for the home than he used to. Aside from candle molds, he makes bread and pie pans, milk pans, strainers and butter churns. In addition, he makes candleholders and punched lanterns. And in the

At the tinsmith's

winter, people would be very uncomfortable without his foot warmers.

The inside of the tinsmith's shop is every bit as noisy as the blacksmith's. There's the banging of the mallet as he shapes tinplate over a mold. There's the piercing squeal of the file which he uses to smooth rough edges. His work requires a good deal of skill and a keen eye for form and shape. Though the metal he uses—thin sheets of iron coated with tin—is light in weight, his work nevertheless takes patience and care. For example, to make a pie tin, the seams have to be folded, soldered, and then the rough edges rolled over wire. And you can well imagine the artistry and patience involved in making a coffeepot with its delicately shaped spout and handle.

The Potter

Here is where the potter works. When he's working at his potter's wheel it's like watching a magician. He's just placed a wet lump of clay on the wheel. As it spins around between his hands, it starts to rise up and up, and suddenly out comes an earthen mug. But that's only the beginning of the process. If we had the time, we could watch him apply the protective glaze which gives it color and sheen. Then, after he has shaped and glazed a number of mugs, dishes, pots and jugs, he fires up his kiln. The kiln is a huge oven, the size of a small room, and it takes a tremendous amount of wood to heat it to the proper temperature.

Potter at work

The pottery is baked in there for several days before it's ready.

The Village Store

Visiting the village store is always an exciting occasion for young and old alike. It gives villagers a chance to catch up on the local gossip as well as bits of national news. But far better, the store has so many fascinating items. Many of them are too expensive for most villagers to buy, but even so, it's fun to look at them.

There are some rolls of cotton cloth and cotton yarn. There's gleaming china and glassware, which only the richer villagers have in their homes. And there's always the delicious aroma of spices from the Indies along with the scent from the kegs of rum, which the men love to sniff. In the way of other foodstuffs, there is wheat flour, which few villagers buy, and the sparkling sugar loaves, which few can resist. You will notice that buyers seldom pay cash for their purchases. Ready cash is a rarity for most, so the storekeeper more often trades his merchandise for a farmer's produce. But now let's get back to the farmhouse for supper. Tomorrow you're going to visit the school.

In the village store

CHAPTER 6

School Days, Good Old Golden Rule Days...

I hope you won't be too disappointed with the school-house. Even some of the villagers are not proud of it. The windows are leaky, and the benches and desks are poorly made. Many of the older students find the desks so narrow that it's hard for them to do their writing.

And unfortunately, this school is no different from most others, because too many farmers are stingy about the money needed in order to have good schools. Most of them agree that every child is entitled to a free education—although, unfortunately, they exclude Indians and slaves. In order for the towns to raise money for schooling, they have to tax each farmer's property. So property owners try to make sure that as little as possible is spent on school buildings, equipment and teachers' salaries.

There is no law, such as we have, which requires every child to go to school. Some parents take advantage of this. Furthermore, district schools are sometimes located too far away for children to attend. In other instances, poor farmers who cannot afford to pay a tax, and families who do not own property, are not allowed to send their children to school. So you can see that too many children, especially poor children, never enjoy the advantages of an education.

The school is small, considering it must accommodate children of all ages. But since all the students do not attend school at the same time, it's seldom overcrowded. For example, our farmer's children are planning to attend school only for the next few weeks. After several weeks at home, they'll return for another brief session. In this way they can keep up with the work at home and on the farm. Most of the villagers believe that ten or twelve weeks of schooling a year is enough, especially for the very young ones.

The inside of the schoolhouse, as you can see, consists of just one room, and not a large one at that. But when it's cold and windy, this small size is an advantage. The more students crowded together, the warmer they'll be, especially those who can't sit close to the fire. There are days when the ink in the inkwells freezes!

The schoolroom is not a very quiet place. The older students recite their lessons to each other, the teacher drones away to another group, and the very young children are seldom silent.

There's only one teacher for the entire school. His job is to instruct everyone, from the youngest on up. Unfortunately, few of the teachers are properly trained to do the task. The town school committee, which is responsible for hiring teachers, is far more interested in saving money than in a teacher's ability. All they ask is that a teacher know how to read and write, some simple mathematics, and a bit of geography. It is important, however, that he be approved by the village minister.

This school is fortunate, at the present time, to have a teacher who is patient, kind, and very much liked by his students. Recently he brought his own globe to school in order to make geography more interesting.

Too many teachers make schooling a dull routine and, in many instances, a most unpleasant experience. One New England teacher, who wishes to improve the village schools and ways of teaching, described his early school days in the following way. He started school at four years of age and found his teacher to be a cranky old man who never had a kind word for any of his students. Worse yet, everyone was terrified of him, as he spent more time and energy punishing than teaching! This is how his former pupil remembers those days:

> I could not think calmly—I could not learn!
> I hated him! I dreaded the time of returning
> day—of nine o'clock—for then I must turn
> to my daily terror.

Schoolmaster in schoolroom

He endured this for several miserable years when, much to his and the other children's joy, this teacher left, but for a frightful reason. He had hit a pupil so hard with a ruler that the child was blinded in one eye. Fearing that he would be expelled, he resigned instead. Another teacher was hired, and all the children looked forward to his coming with a great sense of relief:

He came—he was a cross, sour-looking man, and bawled out at the moment he entered, in a voice more like an ass than a man—"Take your seats, you scoundrels! Is this the way your former teachers have learned you to behave at their entrance?" We fled we knew not whither, like sheep before the wolf! We soon found by experience that we had gained nothing by losing our other tyrant. Some were unmercifully beaten for trifles, others for nothing. If the young writers at any time left a letter, or letters, out of their writing, they were severely punished with the ferula [ruler]; and the number of blows commonly corresponded with the number of letters wanting. In short, our new teacher was worse than the old: he was not only severe, but cruel, and unreasonable.

Fortunately, this teacher was replaced after a few years. The next teacher proved to be quite the opposite. As more and more parents take a greater interest in what goes on at school and become less concerned with saving on school funds, there will be improvements in the future. But like so many changes for the better, this will take time.

The villagers have very firm beliefs in the purpose of schooling. Knowing how to read and write are necessary and useful, but, they believe, meaningless, unless a child learns how to behave like a good Christian.

☞ Children, obey your parents in the Lord : for this is right. Honour thy father and mother, (which is the first commandment with promise,) that it may be well with thee, and thou mayest live long on the earth.

The Sum of the Ten Commandments.

WITH all thy foul love God above.
  And as thyfelf thy neighbour love.

Our Saviour's Golden Rule.

BE you to others kind and true,
  As you'd have others be to you.
And neither do nor lay to men,
Whate'er you would not take again.

A page from a schoolbook

The first exercise of the day, therefore, is for the older pupils to read aloud from the New Testament. The Bible is used to instruct children of all ages in reading, and there is a state law requiring every pupil to learn and recite the catechism daily.

Let's look about the classroom and see what's going on. A group of little children, sitting on benches, are copying out letters and words on their slates from Noah Webster's Blueback Speller. None of them can read yet, but teachers think that the way to start them off is to have them copy and memorize.

Notice that the oldest pupils are using the same textbook. It's the only one used in the school.

Pages from the book would strike you as odd and puzzling. The stories on the left-hand page and on the bottom of the right are lessons in behavior. Most of the stories throughout the text are intended to teach the reader the difference between good and bad behavior. Many others are about patriotism.

Here is something that you'll find almost impossible to believe: no one ever graduates or gets a diploma! School comes to an end when a child's parents think he's learned enough to get along. Or, in some instances, when the student becomes so bored or disgusted with school that he prefers to spend all of his time working at home, or farming, or learning a trade.

There are no high schools where young people can continue their education. The few families who can afford it send their sons, and even their daughters, to private schools, called academies, for further learning.

There the boys learn Greek, Latin, history, geography, higher mathematics, and are introduced to literature.

Unless a boy goes to an academy he cannot ever hope to attend a college for a more advanced education, or to become a lawyer, doctor, or minister. A few of the academies are coeducational, but most girls are sent to female academies. There the girls are taught sewing, embroidery, drawing, painting, music, dancing, and a smattering of French and Italian.

Girls from wealthy families who attend a girls' academy cannot go on to college, because no college admits women. So no girl can ever hope to become a doctor, lawyer, or minister. Since women are not even permitted to vote, they cannot take part in politics.

However, there are a few women who are trying to improve education for girls. For example, there's Miss Sarah Pierce down in Litchfield, Connecticut. A few years back she started a girls' academy which is most unusual. Instead of learning only sewing, dancing and such "ladylike" things, the girls study history, geography, arithmetic, chemistry and other subjects. And Miss Pierce found the history textbooks so dull and inadequate that she wrote and published one herself. This accomplishment must come as a surprise to many of the menfolk who have such a low opinion of women's intelligence.

Then there's Miss Emma Willard, who has a girls' academy in Middlebury, Connecticut. Since women aren't allowed to attend college, she is trying to offer her pupils courses which measure up to college standards. In order to do this she asked permission to attend classes at Middlebury College so that she could study their teaching methods. Sad to say, she was not even permitted to sit in on a few of the classes. Nevertheless, her school is setting a good example and doing well.

Fortunately, within twenty years the schooling system is going to be so much improved that many more children will be able to get a free education.

But enough about schooling. Tomorrow I'm going to take you on a trip to a town that's almost a day's journey from here, and we must leave early.

CHAPTER 7

By Stagecoach to an Industrial Village

I purposely didn't tell you what time I'd have to awaken you this morning. I was afraid you might have turned down the exciting chance to travel by horseback and then by stagecoach, to Pawtucket, Rhode Island, to visit a yarn mill. The truth is it's only quarter to four and we must be ready to leave shortly. One of our farmer's friends, who owns the largest house and farm in the village, is picking us up.

In fact I hear the horse cantering up the road, and we must not keep our friend waiting. You've probably never ridden a horse before, but don't let that worry you. I'll boost you up behind the rider, and all you have to do is hold on tightly to his waist. Besides, his horse has a gentle trot and it's only an hour's journey to the tavern, where we'll get the stage.

THE TURNPIKE

We're going to be traveling in the stagecoach for about forty miles. That probably doesn't seem like much of a distance to you. An automobile could cover it easily in less than an hour. But it is going to take us over seven hours by coach!

You won't find the road very smooth and firm, because the turnpikes are what are called "natural" roads, rather than "artificial" ones, which are surfaced with gravel. The turnpikes have deep ruts, made by the wheels of carriages, coaches and heavy carts, which sink into the soft ground. After a heavy rain, carriage wheels sometimes bog down to the axles.

In spite of these disadvantages, the turnpike is still a great improvement over the network of little back roads it replaced.

The building of turnpikes in New England started in 1792 and spread like a fever, especially in Connecticut, Massachusetts and Rhode Island. Although most of the villagers are content to stay at home, there's a growing number of citizens who feel differently. Among them are the mill owners and merchants in the larger towns who need to get about as rapidly as possible. Some travel all the way from Boston to New York. In addition, more and more raw materials, such as cotton, are being transported across country to the mills. Farmers close to mill towns and cities are starting to sell their surplus crops and need better roads, too.

Goodness knows how much longer it would have taken us to make this trip to Pawtucket a few years ago without the benefit of the turnpike.

There's the tavern up ahead. The stagecoach, which has come all the way from Springfield, is here already and they're changing horses. You'd better get into the coach if you want to sit next to the driver. There's a seat on either side of him, and one of them is vacant.

This coach is one of the newest. The two rows of seats, behind the driver, are wide enough for three passengers each. There are leather curtains instead of windows. The driver folds them up when the weather is warm. Traveling in the open is pleasant, but in the winter, even with the curtains down, the coach is very drafty and cold.

Here comes our driver to collect the fares from the passengers. It costs two dollars and fifty cents—a huge sum of money for most of our villagers, which is the reason so few of them ever think of traveling.

There will be a number of stops on the way and a change of horses in Chepauchet. Don't get alarmed when the driver has his team gallop full-speed down a hill and the coach sways and bumps about like mad. Stagecoach drivers are known to handle their teams of four with great skill. If you fall asleep, which I suspect you may, I'll wake you up when we come to the turnpike.

We've come to the first tollgate, a huge log, suspended across the road. The tollgate keeper will raise it as soon as the driver has paid him. He is being charged thirty-

BOSTON,
Plymouth & Sandwich
MAIL STAGE,

CONTINUES TO RUN AS FOLLOWS:

LEAVES Boston every Tuesday, Thursday, and Saturday mornings at 5 o'clock, breakfast at Leonard's, Scituate ; dine at Bradford's, Plymouth ; and arrive in Sandwich the same evening.   Leaves Sandwich every Monday, Wednesday and Friday mornings ; breakfast at Bradford's, Plymouth ; dine at Leonard's, Scituate, and arrive in Boston the same evening.

Passing through Dorchester, Quincy, Wyemouth, Hingham, Scituate, Hanover, Pembroke, Duxbury, Kingston, Plymouth to Sandwich.   *Fare,* from Boston to Scituate, 1 doll. 25 cts. From Boston to Plymouth, 2 dolls. 50 cts.   From Boston to Sandwich, 3 dolls. 63 cts.

.N. B. Extra Carriages can be obtained of the proprietor's, at Boston and Plymouth, at short notice.— ☞STAGE BOOKS kept at Boyden's Market-square, Boston, and at Fessendon's, Plymouth.

LEONARD & WOODWARD.

BOSTON, *November* 24, 1810.

An advertisement for a stagecoach

three cents, twenty-five for the coach and two horses and four cents for each additional horse. This may seem like a small sum, but having to pay it every ten miles adds up. Some of the tollhouses, like this one, are located in remote places, and the tollhouse keepers are sometimes robbed during the night.

Now that we've made our last stop, it's time to tell you about Pawtucket. Only six miles from Providence, the capital of Rhode Island, Pawtucket is what I'd call an industrial village. Although some of its people are farmers, a growing number of them work in the mills.

More and more mills and factories are being built in Pawtucket. At the present time there's a nail mill which turns out over a thousand pounds of nails a day. There's a rolling and slitting mill where iron rods are slit to make nails, spikes, and horseshoes, and iron hoops are rolled out for hooping barrels. There's also an oil mill which processes whale and linseed oil. Whale oil is being used more and more nowadays as oil lamps replace candles. Someday soon, let's hope our villagers will be able to enjoy the advantages of such lighting. The fastest-growing mills are the yarn mills, which employ a growing number of people.

The use of machinery to turn out cotton yarn is already bringing about great changes. Within less than one generation from now, the increasing use of machinery to spin yarn and, eventually, to weave cloth, is going to revolutionize almost everyone's way of life, including our own villagers'. For better or for worse, I cannot say. It has already happened in England, where huge mills are scattered all over the countryside. Thousands of men, women and children work in the mills from sunrise to sunset six days a week.

The English mill owners are interested in making their mills profitable and have little regard for the people who work in them. As a result, the workers are too often treated with the same kind of cruelty as slaves are in our country. Let us hope that, as more and more people begin working in the mills here, they will not be treated in such a way.

There is a direct connection between what has been happening in England and the establishment of the Old Slater Mill here in Pawtucket. It was founded by an Englishman, Samuel Slater, who introduced his country's manufacturing methods here.

OLD SLATER MILL

The Old Slater Mill is a rather small building, forty-seven by twenty-nine feet and two and a half stories high. The water wheel, which is in the basement, is the heart of the mill and is turned by the flow of the stream. The wheel provides the power for running the machinery throughout the entire building. This is done by means of shafts, connected to gears and belts.

Waterpower is a wonderful source of energy that neither pollutes the air nor the stream. But it does have serious drawbacks. During summer droughts,

The Old Slater Mill, Pawtucket Rhode Island.
Built by Samuel Slater in 1793, and in which was first
introduced in America the spinning of Cotton by machinery.
(From an Old Print)

Old Slater Mill

when the river slows to a trickle, the mill has to shut down. If there's a spring flood and the river rises high above its banks, the wheel does not function well. And when the river freezes over in winter, someone has to break up the ice and chip it away from the wheel. Clambering over the slippery rocks to get at the huge water wheel is an unpleasant and dangerous task. Some years ago, Samuel Slater ordered some of the boys to do this and they refused. Such disobedience would have been unheard of in England, where workers always do what they're told. In this instance, Samuel Slater himself went out and chopped away the ice, and did so on many other occasions.

THE WORKERS

At the present time there are seventy-six workers in the mill. Forty of them are children, some of whom are six and seven years old, but the majority are over ten. There are twenty-five women and eleven men. Some of the men are foremen, some are mechanics, and others are watchmen and wagon drivers. The unskilled male workers receive a dollar a day, the women fifty cents, and the children about twenty-five cents, although their pay increases with their age.

Payday often is only two or three times a year, and not much money is given out then. The mill owners like to hold onto their cash. To do this they've established a company store where the workers are allowed to charge their purchases of food and other necessities. These charges are deducted from their earnings. Some families are so much in debt to the store that they never receive a cent on payday. I've been told of one unfortunate family, a father and seven children, all of whom work in the mill. The father earns six dollars a week, and his children a total of eight dollars and forty-five cents. From last May to December he's owed the company store almost six hundred dollars and will probably remain in debt for a good while. Mill workers who can keep their farms are not as dependent upon the company store and are better off.

Getting people to work at the mill is not easy. Only those families who cannot make a go of farming will consider working there. So mill owners like Mr. Slater realize that they have to treat their workers with some consideration in order to keep them. Unfortunately, this situation will change as more and more people become dependent on mill work for their livelihood. This has been the case in England.

At the present time, the owners and foremen at the Old Slater Mill find it rather difficult to have a disciplined labor force. Samuel Slater, because of his experience in England, has complained about the difficulties with some of the parents who question the authority of the foremen over their children, and who sometimes keep their children at home when they feel like it.

The Pawtucket villagers working in the mill have been used to working twelve and fourteen hours a day, six days a week, on the farm. They are used to having few holidays and no such thing as a paid vacation. What they find difficult in the mill is not the hard work, but the monotonous way they must keep pace with the machines and the nagging of the foremen to make sure they keep working. Nothing like that was involved in farm work.

The factory bell rings at dawn, announcing the beginning of work. In the middle of the morning, around eight, the bell rings again for breakfast, for which half an hour is allowed. The next half-hour break is at noon, and some of the workers go home for their dinner. The final bell tolls as darkness sets in and work has to stop, because there are no lights in the mill.

THE MACHINERY

Now let's go in and see the mill in action. This is the carding machine, and there are six of them in all. It works very much like the carding machine back at our village. But cotton fibers are far more fragile than wool, and perfecting a machine to card cotton took a long time.

One boy feeds the cotton in at one end. Another boy removes the barrels, filled with the carded cotton, and takes them to the next processing machine. It doesn't take any skill to operate this carding machine, and as long as one is careful not to get his hands caught in one of the rollers, studded with tiny, sharp nails, there is no danger involved. However, when the rollers get clogged with cotton, someone has to clean them with a hand carder, and sometimes he is scratched by the sharp teeth.

The carded cotton goes through several more operations before it's wound onto large bobbins. The bobbins are taken over to one of the eight spinning frames which are lined up side by side. As the machines spin

Slater carding machine

A spinning frame

the cotton into yarn, they make an endless whir and clatter.

The foreman sees to it that there is no interruption in the operation of the machines. If someone has to be excused to go to the privy or for some other reason, there's always a standby to take over. Putting on the bobbins, removing the empty ones, then removing the bobbins of yarn is quite monotonous work to do from five in the morning until seven in the evening. Occasionally a strand will break. Then a child has to tie the broken strands together. To keep this from happening often, a boy walks up and down with a pail, sprinkling water on the floor. This keeps the air moist and helps prevent the cotton from becoming brittle and breaking.

The other machines, called *mules,* spin cotton into finer threads than the spinning frame. A huge carriage of the mule is moved back and forth to stretch the yarn. This has an element of danger: when a thread snaps, a small child has to climb under the carriage to tie the threads together. If the carriage were to move then, the child could lose a hand. So far, however, nothing like this has happened here, since the mule operator is the most skilled worker in the mill. Surprising to note, she is a woman, Hannah Cole, who learned her trade years ago from an English spinner. She is one of the highest-paid workers, and she always gets paid in cash.

The final step in the making of yarn is winding the thread into skeins. The skein-winding machines perform the same function as the hand reel you saw at home, but they are much larger and faster.

The finished skeins of thread are then parceled out to families to be woven into cotton cloth. Both men and women do the weaving at home in their spare time, and are paid by the yard.

WORKING CONDITIONS

There are many rumors about the horrors of mill work, but conditions are not presently that bad. Here and there you can see a group of young girls chatting away. Sometimes they can do needlework, and sometimes the boys are allowed to play outside while the mechanics are repairing the machines. Despite the twirling of the cogs and bobbins and the constantly moving leather belts which turn the machines, there is not much danger of serious injury if the workers are careful.

However, there is an ugly side to mill work. Most foremen are not kind and considerate, even of children. Furthermore, few children ever get a chance to go to school. And working indoors, twelve to fourteen hours a day, is not healthy for them, compared to outdoor farm work. Even though accidents are not frequent, when someone is injured on the job the mill owners are not held responsible. The workers must pay for their medical expenses, and if a person is so badly injured that he cannot work for a long time, or if he is completely disabled, no compensation is paid. Also, there's a growing trend for some of the poor families to have as many children as they can. The more little ones they can put to work in the mill, the more money will be coming in. And as mill machinery becomes larger and more complicated, working conditions will become even more unpleasant, and injuries more frequent.

Today, in our modern world, children are protected by laws. They are not allowed to work in factories, and all of them can and must go to school. Factory workers are protected by laws and by labor unions, if they belong. They no longer have to work six days a week, fourteen hours a day. If they do work more than forty hours a week, they receive overtime pay. And they must be paid with money, whether by check or in cash. Furthermore, they're entitled by law to compensation if and when they are injured. However, I should tell you that the accident rate in our factories is one of the highest in the Western world.

I've finished showing you through the mill, and it occurs to me that you've spent almost your entire time seeing how people work: in the home, on the farm, and in the mill. So let's hurry back to the village and see how villagers relax and entertain themselves in what free time they have.

CHAPTER 8

Games and Other Pastimes

Although holidays are few and far between and work-days long indeed, villagers still have spare time for fun. Often during the winter, and on rainy days in the spring or fall, little work can be done outdoors. And there's always Sunday, when no work is supposed to be done at all.

However, until a few years ago, Sunday did not allow for much pleasurable relaxation. Other than going to meeting (which we call church) in the morning, and once again in the late afternoon, there were rules forbidding almost any kind of amusement. The strictest rules did not allow cooking, making beds, sweeping the house, cutting one's hair, or shaving. One was not permitted to kiss a child, travel, run and scamper, or walk anywhere except to meeting. Obviously dancing, and playing cards or any kinds of games were also forbidden. To see that such rules were obeyed, there were, and still are, elected officials called *tithingmen*. To show you how strict they used to be, George Washington was once stopped and challenged by a tithingman, even though he was the country's President at the time. He was traveling by horseback one Sunday morning when a tithingman appeared and told him he was breaking the law. Washington explained that he had been delayed by bad weather and was on his way to meeting in the neighboring town. Only then was the tithingman satisfied and allowed him to proceed.

Nowadays the Sabbath laws are far less strict. Most villagers look forward to meeting as an enjoyable social event. And the minister tries to make it so. Some of the parishioners have to travel a good distance to attend morning service, and, as there's another in the late afternoon, he makes them welcome to stay all day at his house. In the warm weather he has a table set outdoors and serves food and drink. In the winter they are invited to gather around his fireside. Such get-togethers are a pleasant change, as there's not much time for visiting during the week.

There's a good deal of singing in the religious services. This offers another form of relaxation for the young people, who meet in each other's homes for choir practice on weekday evenings.

The villagers are always fond of gathering together,

and even manage to make social occasions out of certain kinds of work. For example, there are *stone bees*. The men come with their teams of oxen and help a neighbor clear away the stones and rocks in a field he wants to farm. To make this into a lively occasion, the farmer serves rum to all the helping hands. At the end of the day the young men often engage in wrestling matches, jumping contests and foot races.

House and barn raising bees are similar work-together, play-together occasions. The frames of buildings are first assembled and nailed together on the ground. Then they have to be raised into position, which requires a lot of helping hands and muscle. Here, too, the host serves a plentiful supply of rum.

Then there's the *corn husking frolic*. Boys and girls from neighboring farms get together in someone's barn and strip the harvested corn of its outside leaves. Singing, and even dancing, are all part of the day's activity.

Stocking knitting or quilting can be a pleasant social event for the women. They meet at someone's house and chat away as they work. At teatime, coffee, tea, or cider and cookies are served.

Marriages are always great social occasions. They are celebrated in the evening at the bride's house. No invitations are required, and everyone in the village is expected to attend. Rum and spirits are generously served, and young and old take part in the dancing.

Dancing is no longer frowned upon, as it was in

earlier times, and is a very popular activity. Even families of modest means give dances in their homes. What is important is that they make little social distinction between rich and poor. There is, as yet, little snobbishness and they socialize freely. Furthermore, young, unmarried people are allowed far more freedom to get together than is presently permitted in England. Village taverns often have balls which young people attend.

There are some pastimes which occasionally have unfortunate consequences. One of them is called "tavern haunting." During the winter months, especially, when there's idle time, some farmers meet at a village tavern and spend the day drinking together. Some of them run up large debts at the tavern and get into financial trouble. In fact, hard drinking is a problem for a number of the villagers, some of whom are known to run up large bills for liquor at the village store as well. This sometimes means that their families cannot buy the things they need. Many of the people are also quite free in allowing young people, even children, to drink liquor. Needless to say, there are those in the villag who disapprove of so much drinking.

There are a few spectator sports which some of the men go out of their way to see. I am ashamed to describe them because of their cruel and violent nature, but I'll mention them briefly, as I promised I'd always be frank. To date, none of them has ever been held in this village. But some of the menfolk have gone

to a nearby town to see them. One is called animal baiting. A hapless bear or bull is tethered to a stake and a pack of dogs is set upon it. Either the dogs are killed by the beast, or it is torn to bits by the dogs. Another such horrid amusement is cockfighting. Bets are placed on which cock will kill the other the moment they're let loose upon each other.

Another pastime which is undoubtedly unhealthy, especially for the young, is the growing use of tobacco. The smoking of "segars" (cigars) is becoming more and more popular. A while back, a weekly newspaper printed this short but sad item:

"Died in Salem, Master James Verry, aged 12, a promising youth, whose early death is supposed to have been brought on by excessive smoking of segars."

However, many other forms of enjoyment are delightful. Winter sleighing is among them. Farmers with horses hitch them to a sleigh and invite everyone to take turns riding across the snow-covered countryside to the merry accompaniment of the sleighbells.

Hunting is another pastime, which also provides food. A young boy usually starts off his hunting adventures with a bow and arrow and goes after quails, partridges, pigeons and even deer, all of which are in abundance. They are also usually safe from his first

hunting efforts with bow and arrow. When he's a bit older he's allowed to try the flintlock, which usually takes five or six pulls of the trigger before it goes off.

Trapball is one of a number of games that boys play. It's the forerunner of our baseball and involves hitting a ball with a bat. There's a game called *fives* in which a ball is hit against a wall. Leaping is another competitive sport. There are many variations: jumping over a bar to see who can leap the highest, or seeing who can make the greatest number of jumps in succession; or how far someone can leap.

Because girls are considered far too weak and delicate (except when it comes to work) to engage in such active sports, they settle for flying kites, seesawing, and playing blindman's buff.

To pass the long, quiet evenings at home, families often sing ballads and hymns together. The older folk tell children stories, some of which are quite scary. Although most villagers own very few books, those they have are read and reread time and again, and some towns even have libraries where one can borrow books.

I hope that if and when you make a return visit, you'll have time to join the young people in a sleigh ride, or a hunting or fishing expedition, and share one of their famed Thanksgiving feasts. And so you'll always recall this journey with pleasure, here are a few old New England recipes which I've updated a bit so you can make them. I hope you'll enjoy using them.

OLD NEW ENGLAND RECIPES

PUMPKIN PIE

What you need:

2 cups cooked
   pumpkin
⅔ cup brown sugar
   firmly packed
2 teaspoons cinnamon
½ teaspoon ginger
½ teaspoon salt

¾ cup milk
2 eggs
1 cup heavy cream
1 teaspoon vanilla
1 frozen pie crust

What you do:

1. Preheat oven to 325°F.
2. Combine pumpkin, sugar, spices, and salt in mixing bowl.
3. Beat in milk, eggs, cream and vanilla with rotary beater.
4. Pour into thawed pie shell.
5. Bake for one hour (or until knife inserted in center of pie comes out dry).

Serve plain or with cheddar cheese.

APPLE PIE

What you need:

4 large green apples
1 cup sugar
¼ teaspoon salt
½ teaspoon cinnamon
grated rind of ½
  lemon

1 tablespoon lemon
  juice
2 frozen pie crusts
butter
cream
sugar

What you do:

1. Preheat oven to 450° F.
2. Peel, core and slice the apples very thin and make sure you have about 4 cups.
3. In a bowl mix the apples with sugar, salt, cinnamon, lemon rind, and lemon juice.
4. Fill one thawed pastry shell with the apple mixture.
5. Dot with butter.
6. Use the second crust as the top crust: remove it from its pan, place it on top of the filled pie, and seal it to the bottom crust with tines of a fork.
7. Slash top crust in several places with a sharp knife.
8. Bake in preheated 450° F. oven for 10 minutes *only*.
9. Reduce heat to 350° F. and bake 30 to 35 minutes.
10. Five minutes before pie has finished baking, brush top with cream and sprinkle generously with sugar.

Serve warm with cheddar cheese or ice cream.

HOECAKE

What you need:

1 cup water-ground white cornmeal	1 tablespoon melted lard
½ teaspoon salt	1 cup boiling water

What you do:

1. Preheat oven to 375° F.
2. Combine cornmeal and salt.
3. Add lard and enough boiling water to make dough heavy enough to hold a shape.
4. Shape into 2 thin oblong cakes.
5. Place in a heavy, hot, well-greased pan.
6. Bake about 25 minutes.

Serve hot with butter.

HOMEMADE BUTTER

What you need:

    1 pint chilled heavy
      cream

What you do:

1. Pour the cream into a jar and seal tightly.
2. Shake up and down, without stopping, for about 20 minutes.
3. When you see a lump forming, keep shaking until it gets no larger—it's butter.

HERB TEAS

CAMOMILE: Pour 1 cup of boiling water over 5 or 6 dried camomile flowers. After 10 minutes, pour through a strainer and sweeten with honey.

MINT: Pour 1 cup of boiling water over a large handful of dried mint leaves. After 10 minutes, strain and sweeten with honey or sugar.

ROSEMARY: Pour 1 pint of boiling water over 1 ounce of the tips of rosemary leaves. Steep for 10 minutes. Sweeten with honey or sugar.

THYME: Pour 1½ pints of boiling water over 2 large handfuls of leaves. Steep for 10 minutes. Sweeten with honey or sugar.

ROBERT H. LOEB, JR. was born in New York City and grew up in Switzerland, Arizona and New York. After attending Brown and Columbia universities, he pursued a variety of writing-related careers from magazine editor to setting up his own mail order publishing business. The author of fourteen books for children and adults, the most recent of which is *Your Legal Rights as a Minor,* Mr. Loeb and his wife live in Connecticut, not far from Old Sturbridge Village and Old Slater Mill.

Index